OTTERS
UNDER WATER

Jim Arnosky

Penguin Putnam Books for Young Readers

A PaperStar Book, published in 1999 by Penguin Putnam Books for Young Readers,
345 Hudson Street, New York, NY 10014.
PaperStar is a registered trademark of The Putnam Berkley Group, Inc.
The PaperStar logo is a trademark of The Putnam Berkley Group, Inc.
Originally published in 1992 by G. P. Putnam's Sons.
Published simultaneously in Canada. Manufactured in China.
Book design by Nanette Stevenson and Colleen Flis. The text is set in Goudy Old Style.
Library of Congress Cataloging-in-Publication Data
Arnosky, Jim. Otters under water/by Jim Arnosky. p. cm.
Summary: Shows two young otters frolicking and feeding in a pond.
1. Otters—Juvenile literature. [1. Otters.] I. Title. II. Title: Otters under water.
QL737.C25A76 1992 599.74'447—dc20 91-36792 CIP AC
ISBN 978-0-698-11556-9
7 9 10 8

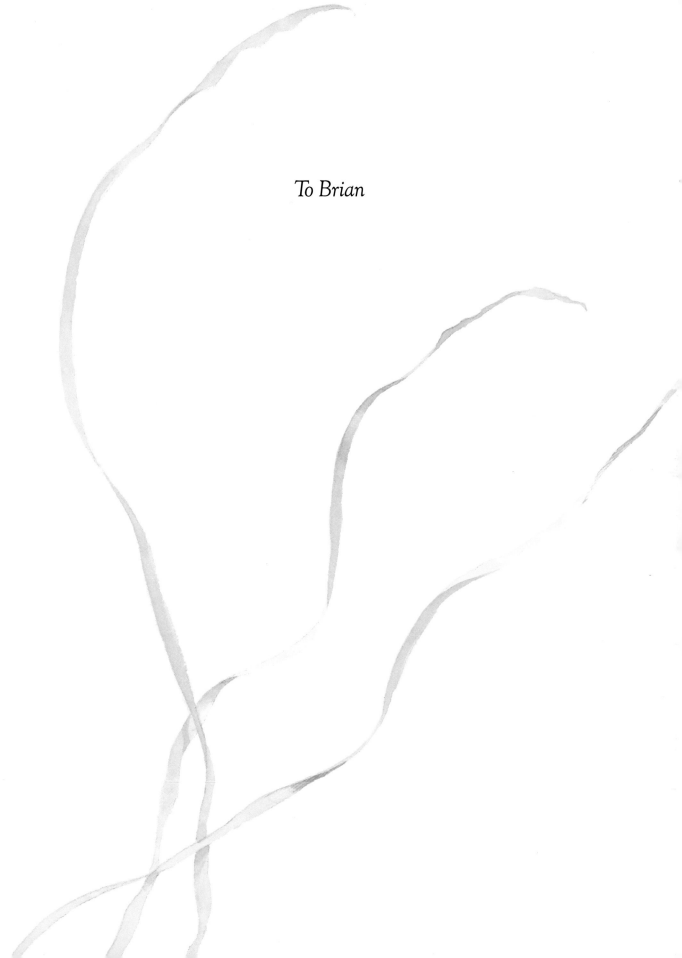

To Brian

It is morning and the sun
is shining softly on the pond.

Two young otters glide by,
making ripples on the water.

From the bank, the mother otter
watches her pups…

swimming side by side,

swimming in a line,

rolling on their backs,

holding their breath,
then diving.

Underwater, they hunt for fish

and crayfish.

They see newts

and snapping turtles.

Otters can hold their breath
a long time. The two sneak
under floating ducks.

They follow slow muskrats.

Otters can swim fast!
One pup chases a yellow perch.

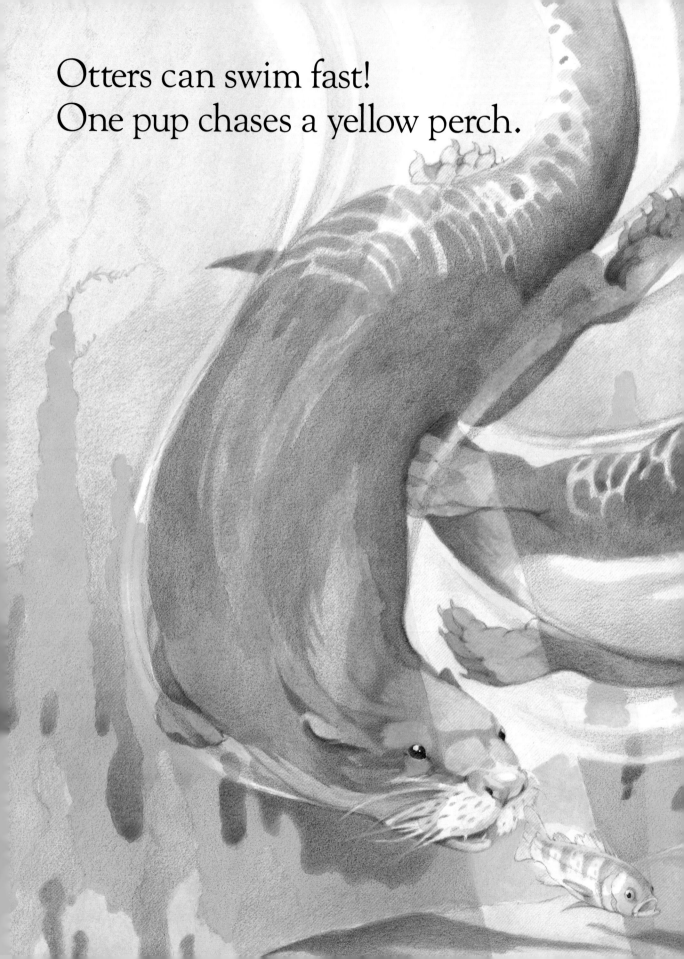

The other pup catches
a silver minnow.

Then, at once, the pups
pop up to the surface to breathe

and find their mother still
watching from the bank.

It is morning and the sun
is shining softly.